S without SELLING

Lessons from the Jungle for Sales Success

TERRI LEVINE

NEW YORK

SELL *without* SELLING

Lessons from the Jungle for Sales Success

By Terri Levine

ISBN: 978-1-60037-464-7 Paperback

Library of Congress Control Number: 2008929655

Published by:

MORGAN · JAMES
THE ENTREPRENEURIAL PUBLISHER™

Morgan James Publishing, LLC
1225 Franklin Ave Ste 325
Garden City, NY 11530-1693
Toll Free 800-485-4943
www.MorganJamesPublishing.com

Cover Wrap & Interior Design by:
Heather Kirk
www.GraphicsByHeather.com
Heather@GraphicsByHeather.com

Habitat for Humanity®
Peninsula
Building Partner

TESTIMONIALS

"The real work started from the inside—replacing old disempowering beliefs with new, life-enhancing ones. This made the outer work easy. Not only did I change my fee schedule to reflect an increase of more than 100 percent, but what has been truly amazing is how easy it's been to attract a new caliber of clients willing to retain my services at this new level."

W. Bradford Swift
Founder, Life On Purpose Institute

Steve Shedroff, *Regional Sales Manager* for a long-term care insurance company, shares his story. He took over an office that was the least productive in his entire company. They were number fifty-four in sales of the fifty-four offices in the company. In eighteen months his team generated so many sales, they moved to number eight in the country, and this year are number one!

"I consider myself marketing savvy; every class gave me new ideas I could use. The energy and enthusiasm you brought to the subject matter made every session a pleasure to listen to. I got eight clients for a teleclass the first week!"

Rosalie Marcus
Lasting Impressions

Laura Barry, *Real Estate agent with Elite Properties*, was not meeting her goal of selling $1 million a year in houses. Using my formula, she sold over $2 million in less than one year and last year out-produced every agent in her office.

"I've been using the tools…I love the system I use and it feels fun and easy for me. Since doing that, I easily attracted four new clients! I'm loving how easy this can be!!!! What I know now is that this program really works!"

Linda Braasch

"I was presenting my new program at a client company. It was a *huge* success, but more important, I was locked on, in that zone, experiencing magic all day!! And to my surprise and delight, I was hired on the spot *and* they asked me to present the same seminar to the company's operation in another city in a few weeks! Thanks for these tools."

Val Williams
Val Williams Professional Coaching and Training, Inc.

TABLE OF CONTENTS

WHAT YOU NEED TO LEARN IN ORDER TO BE SUCCESSFUL IN YOUR BUSINESS

Tips and tactics used by successful salespersons throughout the business world that have been shown to be virtually "bulletproof"

ARRIVAL AT SCHOOL

Standing outside the Krenker Business School of Practical Sales Advice, Christina Richards stood there, taking in the building. It was strong and solid, made of old-fashioned red brick that looked like it had weathered many a storm.

She couldn't believe she was here. Christina was excited to be accepted. She knew she was going to be a success in business. Ever since the first grade she dreamed of having her own business selling art.

Professor Krenker was known as one of the foremost authorities on business, and he was very selective in the kinds of students that he accepted. When she'd spoken to him on the phone, his gruff voice had come through the line loud and clear: "I'm looking for students who want to learn, Miss Richards. I'm looking for students who are going to listen to what I have to say and aren't going to argue with me. I'm looking for students who want to be taught, Miss Richards. Am I making myself clear?"

"Yes, sir," she said emphatically to which the professor responded, "Christina, I hear passion in your voice and a

willingness to learn new things." And with that, the old professor accepted her into his school.

Naturally, there were other sales schools that didn't approve of Professor Krenker. Some said that he was too modern because he didn't believe in using tricks, even dirty ones, to get the job done. Some called him hopelessly old-fashioned because he believed too strongly in the customer and insisted that people sell from the heart as opposed to doing whatever it took to make the sale. Christina just wanted to learn whatever there was to learn about sales so she could begin an art business and sell art done by local artists, and that was all there was to it. She didn't care who she learned from, just as long as she learned what she needed to know. She was passionate about selling art not only because she wanted to help artists get their work known, but she also wanted people to have beautiful paint-ings in their homes.

More than anything, she was determined to be a success.

PROFESSOR KRENKER

*P*rofessor Krenker stood in front of the class and Christina had to smile. He was a little gnome of a man, with white hair going off into several directions, and there was a kind of manic energy about him. As he paced back and forth, there was a sharpness to his gaze as he looked out at the students. Christina sensed there was more to him than met the eye.

"First of all," he said, "I know some of you have probably heard that I'm one of the 'old school' teachers out there. You'll notice that I'm not handing out CDs or DVDs to you or showing you a PowerPoint presentation. What I'm going to do is talk to you. You're going to listen to what I have to say, and you're going to take notes. Then, you'll go home and think about what I've said, and we'll talk about it the following day."

A young man with thick glasses sitting in the front row raised his hand. "Professor Krenker?"

"Yes?"

"Are we going to be tested on what you're teaching us?"

Krenker stared at the student for a moment, then went over and leaned over the student's desk. The student drew back slightly and seemed to shrink into his seat.

"What's your name?" Professor Krenker asked.

"Jonathan Weston."

"Well, Jonathan Weston, you're not here to get a good grade. You're here to get a good understanding of business. Therefore, I'm not going to test you. Either you're going to understand what I'm teaching you or you're not. It doesn't matter to me, either way. I've already been paid to have you here."

Professor Krenker stood up, then, and looked directly at Christina. There was an odd intensity in his gaze. "Now, something that's very important to understand is when it comes to learning about business, I can teach you what knowledge I have, but the wise student will realize I don't have all the answers—but by keeping their eyes open, they'll gain an education in business such as few others have."

Seeing the way that he looked at her, watching his eyes hold hers, Christina had the feeling that Professor Krenker was telling her something important. She didn't know what it was, though.

THE RULER

C hristina went home that night and thought about what Professor Krenker had said. Again, she couldn't help but feel that she had been seeing something in him that the other students hadn't.

"Don't get carried away with yourself, Christina," she muttered, washing her face before she went to bed. "He was just talking."

She crawled into bed, wrapped the covers around herself, and began thinking about her day. She remembered her parents and friends telling her that sales was "a jungle," and her high school business teacher often said, "it's a jungle out there." She wondered what they meant. Did that mean people were tough or the work of selling anything, even something you were passionate about, would be hard? She finally drifted off to sleep after pondering the jungle concept for a while.

Before long, Christina started to dream. All of sudden she found herself standing in the middle of a huge jungle. The sun was shining, the air was warm and pleasant, and the fragrance of tropical flowers tickled her nose.

"Eighteen thousand fifteen...eighteen thousand sixteen... eighteen thousand seventeen..."

Startled by the voice, Christina looked around and noticed an orangutan looking up into a tree and counting. He had a golden crown upon his head and the sight of him was definitely unusual.

"Hello," Christina said.

The orangutan looked at her and frowned. After a moment, he shook his head and approached her.

"You made me lose my place."

"I'm sorry," she said, sincerely. "I was just being polite."

"Do you know how long I've been counting the leaves on that tree?" the orangutan demanded. "Do you have any idea?"

"I'm afraid that I don't."

"I've been doing this for over sixteen hours, and now I've lost count. I'm going to have to start all over."

"But why are you counting leaves?"

He stared at her, surprised. "Because I'm the ruler, of course. This is my jungle."

"Oh. You must have very good eyesight."

"I have the best eyesight in the jungle. I can spot the broken antennae on a butterfly from ten miles away."

"That's very impressive."

"Yes, it is. After all, I am the ruler, and as the ruler, I need to know exactly how much of everything I have. Rulers keep track of everything that they rule over. Now, if you'll excuse me, I have to get back to work."

The orangutan went back to the tree and began to count. Suddenly, a large tree began to rock back and forth, and before Christina could say anything, the tree toppled to the ground, landing less than three feet behind the ruler. Looking up into the tree, he continued to count the leaves there.

"Silly, isn't it?"

Startled once again, Christina turned around and saw a beautiful rainbow-colored bird rising from the branches of the fallen tree.

"Hello," Christina said.

"Hello. Welcome to The Jungle. I'm Bird."

"Hello, Bird. I'm Christina."

"Poor old Ruler," Bird said, shaking her head. "He spends all his times counting the leaves on the trees and never notices when the trees fall down around him. That's the problem with having such good eyesight. Sometimes you can see the littlest things and not see the biggest ones."

LOSING THE BIG PICTURE

The following day, when Christina went to class, Professor Krenker had written on the large whiteboard four words: YOU MUST KNOW EVERYTHING.

The class settled in and Christina found herself remembering the dream from the previous night. It was definitely an odd occurrence, and she couldn't help but feel there was some significance to the dream she wasn't understanding.

Professor Krenker cleared his throat, waited for silence, and pointed to the whiteboard. "Now, then—let's begin with one of the most important rules of selling. If you remember nothing else, you need to remember this, because it's one of the secrets of success that a great many people have failed to take heed of. When it comes to your business, you must know everything about selling your product or service.

"You have to be aware of every facet of your sales as well as any sales force you train and hire, and you need to make sure that it's all running smoothly. You have to have the ability to engage in overseeing everything happening with sales, and you can't ever let up. The moment you let up, you'll find that you're losing ground to your competition."

Christina listened and she frowned. She didn't think Professor Krenker was right.

As if reading her thoughts, the old man's gaze fell upon her, and he slowly approached her. "You have something that you want to say, Miss Richards?"

"I'm not quite sure if I understand what you're saying, Professor Krenker."

"What's confusing you?"

"Are you saying that you need to know everything that's going on with sales?"

He nodded. "Of course."

"And you think you should be doing it personally?"

"No doubt. This isn't something that can be delegated, after all. A good business owner is checking everything there is to check out regarding sales in his or her organization."

She shook her head. "I'm not sure I agree with you."

Several students turned around to look at her, but Christina didn't backtrack. Instead, she took a deep breath and said, "I'm wondering if it's not a better idea to let others help you keep track of sales and other things you can't deal with."

The old man studied her. "And what would be your reasoning for that?"

"Well, I was thinking if you spent all of your time checking on the little things regarding sales, you might find yourself not able to see if some of the bigger things are going wrong."

Professor Krenker stared at her for a long moment, and then he smiled. "You are absolutely correct, Miss Richards. There was a time when many business owners thought they needed to micromanage every little detail of sales in their companies and that led to resentment among the sales force workers as well as a loss of productivity. In the end, by involving themselves with working on the smallest sales details, they lost sight of their overall mission—with serious consequences."

And with that, the old man went to the whiteboard, erased the words and put up new words: DO NOT BE AFRAID TO DELEGATE.

"This is one of the most important lessons you can learn," he announced to the class. "A successful salesperson will know how to delegate tasks and assignments to those working around them. That way, they can concentrate on making sure their business is always on the right track. Remember without selling your product

or service, you won't be in business. To be successful you must create sales."

Professor Krenker nodded at her. "Well done, Miss Richards. I have a feeling you're going to do quite well in this class."

She found herself smiling with delight.

CHRISTINA MEETS SNAKE

*T*hat night, Christina dreamt of The Jungle once again. This time, she was standing at the bottom of a beautiful waterfall. A gentle mist washed over her, refreshing her, making her feel cool and wonderful. Bird flew over to her, landing on her shoulder. Christina laughed with delight. "I don't know why I'm dreaming about this place again, but I'm glad that I am," she said. "It's wonderful."

Bird trilled with delight. "I'm glad you think so. Would you like to come with me and explore some more?"

"Definitely."

Bird flew a short distance ahead and Christina followed. There was a small path she took that moved between magnificent palm trees and short bushes that had red flowers giving off the most delightful fragrance. The path took them to a small clearing where she was surprised to find a crowd of sheep standing in front of a large black snake. Next to the snake was a cardboard box. Christina turned to Bird. "What's going on?"

Bird sighed. "Snake is trying to sell the sheep something. He does this all the time."

They approached Snake. His green-slitted eyes flicked over to them and then went back to looking at the sheep. "You're wondering how I can sell you what's in this box for nothing more than five goldens," Snake said, his voice soft and seductive. "Aren't you?"

A couple of the sheep nodded.

"It's simple. I like you. I like you so much that I'm going to take a loss on this and that's the truth. I know I shouldn't be doing this, but what can I say? Snake is a good judge of character, and I can tell you're going to be good customers."

"What's in the box?" Christina suddenly asked.

Snake turned to her. His eyes narrowed to even smaller slits than they had been. "Who are you?"

"I'm Christina," she said, "and I was wondering what's in the box."

"Hey, yeah," one of the sheep responded. "You haven't told us what's in the box."

Snake looked indignant. "What are you saying? Are you saying I'm trying to sell something that isn't of the highest quality? Snake has never been so insulted!" And with that, Snake slithered away, pushing the box ahead of him with his snout.

The sheep walked away, obviously happy that they hadn't fallen for a trick, but Christina was surprised to find a raccoon left behind. He watched her with merry green eyes and then hopped towards her.

"Name's Raccoon," he said, extending a paw. "How are you?"

"I'm fine," Christina responded.

"I didn't catch your name, I'm afraid."

"Christina."

"Well, Christina, how do you like our little slice of paradise?" he asked.

"I like it very much."

Raccoon nodded. "Yes, it's a rather pleasant place. Well, I don't want to keep you. Enjoy your stay here, and if you need anything, you just let Raccoon know."

And with that he moved off, and Christina turned to Bird. "I like him," she announced.

Bird nodded. "Yes, Raccoon is very likeable. He and Snake are the only two sales animals in the jungle."

Christina was surprised. "Raccoon is in sales?"

"Oh, yes."

"But, he didn't try to sell me anything."

Bird gave her a curious look. "First, he sold you on himself. The rest will come later."

SELLING YOURSELF

When Christina went to class the next day, Professor Krenker stood next to the whiteboard and wrote down in big, bold letters: WHAT IS THE MOST IMPORTANT THING THAT YOU CAN SELL?

One of the students, a young man with thick glasses, raised his hand and the professor nodded at him. "Yes, Mister Peterson. Can I help you?"

"I'd like to answer the question you wrote on the board."

The old man had a slight smile on his face. "You would."

"Yes, sir."

"Well, by all means, let's hear it. What do you think is the most important thing that you can sell?"

Peterson drew himself up and said, in a very self-satisfied tone of voice, "The most important thing that you can sell is a quality product."

Professor Krenker shook his head. "Wrong."

Peterson's eyes widened in disbelief. "What are you talking about, sir? If you don't sell a quality product, people are not going to buy it."

"Oh, really? Are you telling me every product that sells well is quality? I can think of at least a dozen late-night infomercials I know that are not producing quality items."

The student opened his mouth as if to protest and then shut it, shaking his head.

"What is important, Peterson, is having a quality product along with being a person who can sell himself or herself. I don't care how great your product is; if the customer does not feel comfortable with you, they are not going to want to do business with you. It is the blend of the quality of the product and you as a salesperson that creates trust which in turn promotes credibility and boosts sales."

Professor Krenker looked around the class and his gaze settled on Christina. Once again, she had the unmistakable feeling that something was going on in her dreams that she didn't know about.

"Miss Richards."

"Yes, sir."

"Do you think you can tell the class what might be the most important thing that you can sell?"

She thought back to her dream, thought back to Raccoon, and she said, "I think the most important thing that you can sell is yourself, sir."

Peterson snorted, but Krenker shot him a dark look. "That's absolutely correct, Miss Richards," he announced

to the class, looking at each student in turn. "All of you would do well to remember that."

His gaze settled on Christina and he smiled warmly. "To be a good student of sales you must be open to understanding what I'm trying to teach you."

SELLING IS SERVING

C hristina was exhausted after class. She kept thinking about having a quality product and knew the art she would have in her store would be beautiful. She felt comfortable with that, but she wondered about how to create relationships so people liked her and trusted her. She decided to eat a quick dinner and to relax on the sofa and put her mind to rest.

That night, she quickly drifted off to sleep and found herself back in The Jungle and welcomed by Raccoon. "Hi!" she said.

Raccoon instantly smiled at Christina and asked, "How can I serve you today? Surely you've come back to our jungle for something, and I'd really like to be of help to you!"

This confused Christina a bit. She wasn't sure why she returned to The Jungle, and she definitely wasn't sure what Raccoon could do for her. "I really don't know," she said. "I am just confused about a few things and somehow when I am here I seem to get clarity."

Raccoon smiled at Christina and said, "You don't have to know what you want, and you don't have to want anything. It is just a delight having you here and getting the opportunity to be of service to you if I can help."

Christina pondered for a bit, and then it hit her! Raccoon might be able to explain why The Jungle was supposedly so dangerous and scary; after all he lived there. "Raccoon," she started, "I know The Jungle is a dangerous place to be, and you must be frightened sometimes of some of the creatures. Yet you always seem calm, and I never feel that you are scared. It is a jungle after all, so how do you do it?"

Raccoon looked deep into Christina's eyes and said, "my friend, to me it isn't a jungle at all. I just have a positive, open, and friendly mind. I am inquisitive, and I love to rummage around to see who and what is here. Everyone else dumps out garbage and can't see the gifts in what they toss away. I, on the other hand, enjoy all the garbage. I am excited to see new things, meet new people, have new experiences, and to learn more. I am happy to help others find their way and to see the jungle like I do. It is magical and beautiful, and when you choose to see it that way it isn't scary at all! So, Christina, is there anything I can support you with right now?"

Christina felt like she had to digest what she just heard before she could ask for help. She realized she felt calm and was looking forward to seeing the sales jungle as being less of a threat. She wanted to be like Raccoon and enjoy herself, and she wondered how she could be of service in her real world.

"Thanks Raccoon. I got exactly what I needed. You did serve me, and I've decided I will do the same for others."

HIGH PRESSURE MEANS NO SALES

O n her way to class the next day, Christina stopped in at a specialty boutique that was a few blocks away from her apartment. Her best friend's engagement party was coming up, and she wanted to get a new outfit.

One of the things Christina liked about this particular boutique was that the owner was a middle-aged woman who never tried to use any high-pressure tactics on her. She'd been in too many stores where a salesperson would come up and attempt to sell her something that she just wasn't interested in.

Entering the store, Christina was surprised to find a young brunette behind the counter. The girl came rushing over to her and gave her a smile that seemed a little too forced. "Can I help you?" she asked.

"I'm just looking," Christina told her.

"What are you looking for? Maybe I can help."

Christina found herself already getting a little annoyed. "I'll be fine on my own. Thank you."

"Are you sure? If you can just give me a hint as to what you're looking for, I'm sure I can—"

"I'm fine," Christina interrupted her and quickly moved towards the back of the store.

She was looking at a pink blouse that had pearl-colored ruffles along the sleeves she liked and the salesgirl came back, holding up a hideous black skirt that looked like it was made out of burlap.

"How about this?" the girl asked.

Christina stared at the skirt. "What is that?"

"It's on special, and it would actually be perfect for you."

"What makes you think that?"

"It goes with your complexion."

"The only way that would go with my complexion," Christina said, "is if I were being prepared for embalming. Listen, I appreciate the help, but I'm actually fine on my own."

The salesgirl stammered, "but…but, I've learned in class to help my customers, and I'm sure I'm able to show you things that—"

Christina sighed, and put the blouse back on the shelf. "You know what; I think I'll come back some other time. Thanks for your help," and with that, she left.

As she walked down the street, heading to class, she thought about what a horrible experience that had been and how she would never try to sell someone something they didn't want.

DREAMING
OF SNAKE

That night, Christina found herself dreaming once again of The Jungle. She was walking along a path and Bird appeared, landing on her shoulder and playfully pulling at strands of her hair. "Hello, Woman," Bird said.

"Hello, Bird." They walked in silence for a little while, and it was a comfortable silence—the kind of silence that is shared between friends.

The path turned and Christina suddenly found herself in a clearing. Tall trees were all around, but there was one small area where nothing grew.

In the center of this natural circle, Snake was talking to a large Stork.

"I am looking for some perfumed oil," Stork said. "I have company coming, and I want everything to be perfect."

Snake hissed out a laugh. "You don't want perfumed oil," Snake told Stork. "What you want is some fresh meat for a stew."

Bird whispered to Christina. "Snake has too much fresh meat that he needs to get rid of. He's going to try to make Stork buy it."

Stork shook her massive bill and said, "I don't want fresh meat. I want perfumed oil."

"What good is perfumed oil if your guests are hungry, Stork? What kind of hostess are you going to be if your guests come over to visit and you don't have fresh meat for them? Do you want others to start saying, 'Oh, that Stork— she has a place that smells real nice, but she don't have no food for her guests.' Is that what you want them to say?"

Stork looked uncertain. "I…I'm not…I don't know what I want," she said.

Snake nodded, and when he spoke, there was compassion and understanding in his voice, "I understand, Stork. You got company coming, and you're not sure what you want to do. You're being pulled in all different directions. What you need to do is buy some of this fresh meat, go home, and then make a good stew for your company. No one ever felt bad about having a good meal, you know."

"That's true," Stork said, uncertainly.

"Of course, it's true. Snake doesn't lie."

Christina looked at Bird. "What Snake's doing is terrible! Stork doesn't even want the fresh meat."

Bird sighed, "It doesn't matter. Sometimes, Snake will rollover anyone until they buy whatever he's selling."

"But that would make me want to stop doing business with Snake."

Bird gave her a knowing look. "There are always going to be customers for Snake, but each year there are less and less."

10
FAREWELL TO
THE HARD SELL

*I*n class the next day, Professor Krenker stood in front of everyone and said, "More and more, we're finding there are new methods that are being used to sell, and they are replacing the old methods. Although there are some who still insist upon using techniques that are outdated, they will find some small measure of success. However, those methods will work less and less effectively, and the time will come when they're not useful at all. Can anyone suggest a technique that no longer works with today's consumer?"

Christina raised her hand. "Yes, Christina. What are your thoughts?"

"I was thinking about the 'hard-sell' approach. I was in a store yesterday, and the salesgirl kept trying to get me to buy this really hideous skirt."

Professor Krenker laughed. "Believe me; I've been there with you. You might not think that men have to go through the same thing as women, but the truth is if a man walks into any electronics store and attempts to buy something, a salesperson is going to come along and attempt to sell him something he absolutely does not want. It'll either be a high-priced item or else it will be some kind of useless warranty that'll be a waste of money."

Peterson raised his hand. Professor Krenker nodded at him. "Yes, Mister Peterson. What would you like to say?"

"Sir, with no disrespect intended, I have to differ with you. From what I've seen of the hard-sell technique, it definitely is effective. I've seen figures that show hard sell will have a 50 percent success rate among the right demographics."

The professor chuckled, "I'm willing to bet the figures that you saw, Mister Peterson, were produced by some old-fashioned salesperson who is attempting to market their technique as being useful. Yes, I'm sure there are still people who have caved beneath the hard-sell pressure, but the fact is, those customers will never do business with that salesperson again. People do not like the hard-sell approach. It's just not effective."

"But if you make enough big commissions, doesn't that make it worthwhile?"

Professor Krenker shook his head. "Of course not. The best way to make sure your customer base continues to grow is to make sure you've made the buying experience as pleasant as possible. If you use the hard-sell approach on someone, how many people do you think would recommend you as someone to do business with?"

Peterson shook his head. Christina could tell that he still didn't understand the things the professor was trying to teach them.

"Christina," the professor suddenly said, "how would you attempt to sell an item that wasn't selling?"

Christina thought about it for a moment. "I'm not sure. I guess, if I were a salesgirl, the first thing I'd do is find out what the customer was looking for and see if there wasn't some way to introduce the item I wanted to sell. But, if the customer wasn't interested, I'd just have to let it go."

The old man nodded. "Exactly. Better to keep a customer than to make an unwanted sale. Always remember that."

BELIEVE IN THE PRODUCT

A couple of days later, Christina got a phone call from her Uncle Vinnie. It was totally unexpected, and she was immediately on her guard. Her uncle was notorious for being involved in "get rich quick" schemes, none of which ever worked out.

"Christina, your mother told me that you're studying business stuff," Uncle Vinnie said. "I think I might have a job for you."

"That's very nice, Uncle Vinnie, but—"

He cut her off. "Look, I can't talk right now. I'm going to drop by later on, and I'll show you what I've got. You're going to love this. It's going to make us a lot of money." He hung up before she could protest.

Christina sighed. The only way out of this that she could see was to simply not answer her phone, but sooner or later, she knew that Uncle Vinnie would track her down, and she'd be forced to deal with whatever it was that was on his mind.

She prepared herself for the worst. Two hours later, Uncle Vinnie showed up. He was wearing a suit that had definitely seen better days, but then again, Uncle Vinnie himself had seen better days. His eyes were shiny and dark, and as he came into her apartment, Christina had a sudden memory of Snake in her dreams.

Sitting down on her couch, Uncle Vinnie gave her a bright smile, but the smile didn't quite reach his eyes.

"How are you, Uncle Vinnie?"

"I'm fine. Fine. Right now, I'm sitting on a gold mine, and I thought that I'd invite my favorite niece to share in my good fortune."

"I tried to tell you on the phone that I wasn't—"

He took out a green bottle and set it on the coffee table. "Christina, what's the number one problem in the world today?"

She thought for a moment. "Pollution? Global wars? Diseases?"

Uncle Vinnie shook his head. "Wrong—wrinkles."

"Wrinkles?"

Uncle Vinnie nodded, and there was an excited gleam in his eyes. "Yes! Everyone worries about wrinkles, and what I've got in that bottle is worth a fortune. I'm letting you in on the ground floor of a major business opportunity."

"Wrinkles," Christina repeated.

"Right. Wrinkles. In this bottle, there are secret herbs

and a special kind of water that will eliminate wrinkles in six weeks."

Despite herself, Christina reached for the bottle and uncorked it. She took a sniff and made a face as a horrible odor reached her. "Ewww! What's in here?"

"Can't tell you that. It's a secret."

"It smells awful."

"Sure, it smells awful. That's how people know that it's good."

"Uncle Vinnie, what are you trying to pull here?"

He gave her a hurt look. "What do you mean?"

"I have a feeling something's going on that you're not being upfront about."

He stared at her for a long moment and nodded. "Fine. Here's the deal. I want to do an infomercial, and I want you to help me produce it. I want it to run late at night when you got a bunch of old women watching who are worried that they look like mummies."

Christina stared at him. "You're not serious."

"Of course I'm serious. Why wouldn't I be?"

"You're asking me to sell something I'm sure I wouldn't believe in."

"What's wrong with that?" he asked. "You think the President of Coca-Cola believes in Coca-Cola? He believes in making money. That's all."

"Uncle Vinnie, I'm sorry. I have a desire to sell art. I can't bring myself to sell something I don't believe in. It's wrong."

He stared at her in astonishment. "You're never going to make it in the world of business, kid, that's for sure."

MAGIC WATER

That night, Christina found herself back in The Jungle again. Walking down a path with Bird flying ahead of her and occasionally alighting on a branch, she felt peaceful and alive. It was a welcome relief after her conversation with Uncle Vinnie.

The path turned and led into a clearing. She saw Snake in the middle of the clearing, and next to Snake was a large warthog. On the ground, there were several vials of what looked like muddy water. Bird flew to a nearby branch and laughed. "Snake's at it again," she said. "He never gives up."

"What's he doing now?"

"Watch him," Bird suggested.

Christina stood nearby and watched as Snake went in front of Warthog and said, "Do you want to know why I called you here, Warthog?"

"I was sleeping in the shade. Why did you have to disturb me?"

"Because I found something I just knew you had to have, Warthog. I found something that you've been looking for your entire life."

"And what's that?" Warthog snorted, his voice thick with suspicion.

Snake looked around, as if to make sure he wasn't going to be overheard, and he said in a loud whisper, "I can make your dreams come true, Warthog."

"What dreams?" Warthog demanded.

"The dreams that every warthog has," Snake said, smoothly. "I can make you fly."

There was a moment of stunned silence, and then, Warthog burst into laughter. "That's a good one, Snake. You almost had me there."

Snake reared back and did his best to try to act offended. "What you are talking about? Are you suggesting that I was trying to cheat you?"

"Why would a warthog want to fly, Snake? We don't have wings. I think maybe you've been drinking too many of your own potions."

Snake slithered over to where the vials were and paused. "Inside these glass tubes is the magic water all birds drink. Every night, before they go to bed, they make sure to drink some of what's in these tubes so they can fly in the morning."

Warthog frowned. "But birds fly because they have wings."

"That's right— and that's because they drink the magic water that makes them grow wings, of course."

"Birds are born with wings," Warthog challenged.

Snake laughed. "That's what the birds tell everyone but the truth is, does anyone really know? Of course not. When the eggs are hatched, the birds are high-up in a nest where no one can see them. Then, the mother bird gives the baby birds some of this magic water, and the next thing you know, they have wings and they're flying."

Warthog opened his mouth then closed it.

"Of course," Snake continued, "if you're not interested, I can let some other warthog have the magic juice. Then, you can look up in the sky and see the other warthogs flying around, and you'll be the one stuck on the ground while everyone else laughs at you."

Warthog stared at Snake for a long moment, and then said, "How much is the magic water?"

Christina turned to Bird, astonished. "Doesn't Warthog know he'll never be able to fly?"

Bird was silent for a few seconds, and when she spoke, there was a great sadness in her voice. "When it comes to having dreams, sometimes we don't want to face the truth about certain things."

REPEAT CUSTOMERS

*T*he following day in class, Professor Krenkle decided to explain to the students about the importance of "repeat customers."

Standing in front of his students, the old man looked out at them and said, "If you're going to be a success in business, you need to understand the importance of getting repeat customers. Now, who can tell me the best way that you can build up a repeat customer base?"

Peterson's hand shot up. For some reason, Peterson was always anxious to answer the questions, Christina noticed, even though a great many times, he simply didn't seem to know what he was talking about.

Professor Krenkle looked around, as if hoping someone else would raise his or her hand, but when no one else appeared to be forthcoming, he sighed and said, "Yes, Mister Peterson. Could you please tell the class the best way of getting repeat customers?"

"Sure. You need to sell a product that they have to keep using."

Krenkle thought about that for a moment. "Yes," he finally said, "that's one way you can do it, but—"

"Professor, let's face it. If you go out there and you're selling something that gets used up, it's only natural they're going to keep coming back to you. That's common sense."

"True, assuming that the product you're selling actually is useful," the old man said.

Peterson frowned. "What do you mean?"

"Well, if you're selling something that's useless, you're not going to have many repeat customers, are you? Once someone realizes that something isn't working, what in the world makes you think they're going to continue buying from you? I don't care how much they like you."

Peterson smiled, and there was something familiar about the smile, Christina realized, but she wasn't sure what it was. "Professor Krenkle, surely you've got to realize that people are really naïve. If you're a business person, it's your job to make sure that people keep coming back to you, right? The only way they're going to do that is if you make sure they understand that you're important to them."

"Ah Mister Peterson, it's really the other way around. Your customer should know that *they* are important to you."

Peterson shook his head. "No way. That's old-fashioned thinking, professor."

"There's nothing old-fashioned about taking care of your customers, Mister Peterson."

"I'm just saying that the best way to keep your customer coming back is to make sure you're selling something they're going to want to use and that has to be constantly replaced. If it is something they buy once and never come back for more or never tell their friends about it you won't have a lot of business."

Christina raised her hand. "Yes, Christina? You have something that you want to add?"

Peterson turned to look at her, and she saw that there was something familiar about his eyes, too, but again she couldn't quite figure out what it was.

She forced her attention to Professor Krenkle. "Yes, sir. I wanted to say I don't think it's right that you would try to sell something to a customer just for the sake of having them come back and buy it again and again. I think the product should be something you believe in. It's like what you said earlier. A customer has to believe in both the product and the sales person."

"You're absolutely right," the professor responded.

Peterson rolled his eyes. "It's easy to see which of us here are going to succeed," he said, in a loud whisper, "and which of us are going to fail." The class laughed, and Christina felt her face heat up.

Professor Krenkle's only response was to look at Peterson with a displeased expression on his face.

TRY IT AND YOU'LL LIKE IT

When Christina got home from school, she found Uncle Vinnie standing outside her door. She sighed, shaking her head, and wondered just what it was going to take to get the man to leave her alone. "Uncle Vinnie," she said, "what are you doing here?"

He gave her a smile, and even though she knew that he intended for it to be warm and reassuring, it came across as somewhat predatory. "I just thought that I'd stop by and find out if you'd changed your mind about what we talked about the other day."

"You mean, if I wanted to help you sell that product of yours?" she asked, unlocking the door.

He nodded. "Right."

"I'm still not interested," she told him.

She went inside, and he followed her. Christina wondered just how in the world she was going to get rid of him.

They went into the living room, and Uncle Vinnie sat down on the couch. He gave her a long look, and Christina finally said, "Uncle Vinnie, I'm not—"

He held up a hand. "Before you say another word, there's something that I think you should consider," he told her.

"What's that?"

"Didn't they teach you in business school or wherever it is that you're going that before you jump to the wrong conclusion that you should find out for yourself whether or not something is worthwhile?"

"Yes, but—"

"In that case," he said, taking a small jar of face crème from his jacket pocket, "I want you to try it."

"But I don't have any wrinkles, Uncle Vinnie. It wouldn't be a valid test."

"How can you say that? All you need to do is put this face crème on, and then you can tell whether or not you feel a difference. It doesn't just get rid of wrinkles, you know. It's a great moisturizer, and it's a terrific acne preventative."

Christina almost continued to argue with him, but she realized that if she did, she was never going to get rid of him. So, instead, she picked the small jar and nodded. "Fine. I'll try it, Uncle Vinnie."

He gave her a big grin. "That's all that I ask."

"But, I'm warning you right now," she told him, "that if I don't feel any difference, I'm not going to help you with

marketing this. In fact, I'm probably not going to help you market it in the first place. But, the least I can do is see what I think about it."

He nodded. "That's all I ask. You just try this, and you'll see I know what I'm talking about."

Somehow, Christina had the feeling that no matter what she said, it was going to be very difficult to get rid of Uncle Vinnie.

CLOUD POWDER

When Christina dreamt of The Jungle again, she found herself walking down a familiar path, the one that led to the clearing where she'd watched Snake sell Warthog the magic potion that would supposedly enable him to fly.

She looked in the air and watched as Bird approached. The small creature did a joyous double loop and landed on a nearby branch. "Hello, Christina," Bird said.

"Hi, Bird. You looked like you were having fun just now."

Bird trilled out a merry tune, her small head nodding. "I am. I love flying. I love the wind under me and the ground below. I love racing the clouds."

"That sounds nice," Christina said, but Bird heard hesitation in her voice.

Bird gave her a long look, head cocked to one side. "Isn't there something that makes you feel that way?" Bird asked.

Christina thought for a moment and then said, "Yes! Ever since I was a young girl I wanted to sell beautiful paintings and to decorate people's home with them!"

Bird said excitedly, "So you like art as much as I like flying!"

Christina smiled. "I do! And I understand now, Bird. Flying makes *your* heart sing, and I know that working with art and artists will make mine sing as well."

Bird nodded. "It's always joyous to do what you love."

With that, Christina started walking in silence but this time with a definite bounce in her step. Bird flew slightly ahead of her, and once again they found themselves in the clearing.

Snake was there as was Warthog. Warthog looked very upset, and it was obvious that Snake was doing his best to keep the large animal calm to prevent it from trampling him. Bird let out a musical laugh. "Looks like Snake might be having some problems with Warthog."

Christina grinned. "I guess Warthog finally figured out that the magic water wasn't going to make him fly."

The two of them stood near enough to hear the conversation taking place. "You lied to me, Snake," Warthog said, angrily. "That wasn't magic water that you sold me."

Snake did his best to look utterly indignant. "How can you possibly say that?" he asked, his voice hurt and shocked. "What makes you think it wasn't magic water?"

"Because I haven't been able to fly," Warthog snapped.

Snake looked confused. "You've been practicing, right?"

"Of course I've been practicing."

Snake shook his head. "I don't understand. It definitely should work. Unless…" he said, and his voice trailed off.

Warthog narrowed his eyes. "Unless what?"

"Well, once in a while, the magic water doesn't work the way that it's supposed to work. Usually, it's because the person who is using it happens to have such an intelligent and strong personality that it dilutes the magic inside the water. I should actually have realized that someone like you wouldn't have been able to use just the magic water."

"What are you trying to pull?" Warthog demanded.

Snake shook his head. "I'm not trying to pull anything, Warthog. Didn't I just get through telling you that the magic water didn't work because you're too intelligent? Do you think I'd try to put something over on someone obviously smarter than I am?"

For a moment, Warthog looked confused, and then a look of smug satisfaction appeared on his face. "No, you wouldn't."

"Of course I wouldn't," Snake said.

"So what can I do, then?"

Snake appeared to think for a long moment, and then he nodded. "There is one thing that will possibly help."

"What's that?"

"I have some Cloud Powder that you can sprinkle on yourself. It's made from the rarest of the clouds in the sky, and it's lighter than anything you can imagine. It's possible that if you use the Cloud Powder, along with the magic water, that you might be able to get off the ground."

"Where is this Cloud Powder?" Warthog demanded.

"I have it back at my house," Snake said. "Why don't you come with me and I'll give you some?"

Christina watched as Snake and Warthog headed down a path, and she turned to Bird, astonished. "How does Snake do that?" she asked.

Bird whistled out a little sigh. "It's easy to sell a dream," she said, "but it's harder to sell the truth."

DOING RIGHT BY THE CUSTOMER

*T*he following day in class, Professor Krenkle began to explain to the students about the importance of doing right by the customer. Pacing back and forth, the little man said, "Right now, we're living in an age where customer service is becoming a thing of the past. People are paying more and receiving less personalized attention, and it's becoming a cold way of doing business.

"Now, you might think that because there are fewer and fewer businesses who are worried about customer service that gives you the right to deliver less in that area yourself. Nothing could be further from the truth. In fact, even though we have less customer service than ever, those companies that provide good customer service are doing more business than ever before."

Christina raised her hand.

"Yes, Christina?"

"How can you tell if you're delivering good customer service?" she asked.

Professor Krenkle smiled. "Right. There is an excellent question. If you ask many business owners if they believe they're providing good customer service, you'll find that most of them believe they're doing a good job. However, if you go to their customers, you'll find the exact opposite. That's because many businesses don't actually undertake the arrangements to find out if they are doing right by their customers.

"One of the best ways to make sure that you're keeping up with customer service is to make sure that your customer can reach you when they need to—and this means answering your telephone, responding to an e-mail, writing a letter back to the customer. Keep in mind that in today's market, one of the best selling points for a business is if the customer knows that when they call on the telephone, they are going to speak to an actual person. That's worth more than you can possibly imagine."

A young woman in the second row raised her hand. "Yes, Miss Leonens," Professor Krenkle said. "What can I do for you?"

"I just wanted to let you know that I couldn't agree more about customer service. One thing that drives me crazy with businesses today is that they make all these promises, but they won't, or don't, deliver."

The professor nodded. "An excellent point. When a customer contacts you and you tell them that you are going to do something, it's important that you keep your word. This doesn't mean that you should *try* to keep your word.

It means that you *keep* your word. If you can't, because of some unforeseen situation, you then do whatever it takes to make sure that you can fix the problem."

Peterson raised his hand and Professor Krenkle sighed. "Yes, Mister Peterson. What is it this time?"

"Well, sir, I was just thinking that if a company spends all of its time dealing with customer complaints, they're not going to have time to grow and expand—and everything in business relies upon growth and expansion."

"Mister Peterson, if you're worried about doing nothing but spending time dealing with customer complaints, I have a feeling that you're doing something wrong with your business."

"I'm just saying that from what I've read, everything in business relies upon growth. Sure, you might lose a few people here and there, but I've observed that you're always going to have a certain number of core people who are going to be with you, no matter what."

"That's not quite true, though," Professor Krenkle said. "The moment that a business concentrates on quantity over quality, it begins a downward descent. At some point, another business will come along with comparable prices to whatever you are charging. If they offer better customer service, word will get out, and you'll find that you've lost your customer base."

Peterson looked less than convinced.

17
TRYING OUT THE FACE CRÈME

W hen Christina got home from class, she found there was a message from Uncle Vinnie, wanting to know her thoughts on the face crème that he'd given her. She'd been putting off trying it for as long as possible, but there was nothing more that she could do. She knew that the man wouldn't leave her alone until she'd actually used it and gotten back to him, so she found the jar and put some on.

Even though it was a face crème, Christina just couldn't bring herself to put something on her face that she knew nothing about—and that had come from Uncle Vinnie. Instead, she just placed some on the back of her hand and sat down to catch-up on reading some of her e-mails that had been piling up.

Ten minutes later, she realized that something was happening to her hand. She looked down at it and saw that it was getting red; there was also a distinct itching feeling coming over the entire area.

Christina wasted no time. She rushed to the kitchen sink and furiously washed her hands. Unfortunately, it seemed as if the water caused some kind of reaction with the crème; the itching grew even worse, and the redness got more intense.

Just then, the telephone rang. Doing her best not to itch her hand, Christina answered the phone and found Uncle Vinnie on the other end of the line. "So, how's my favorite niece?" came his booming voice.

"Your favorite niece is not doing so well right now, Uncle Vinnie. I just tried out that crème of yours."

"Yeah? Amazing stuff, isn't it?"

"If 'amazing stuff' is another way of saying that the crème is a hazardous product and should be disposed of by trained professionals, I'd have to agree with you."

There was a pause. "What are you talking about?"

"I'm talking about the fact that I'm having some kind of horrible reaction to it, Uncle Vinnie. How could you do this to me?"

"What are you saying? I thought that—"

"No, you didn't think at all. You just saw a way to make some money and you decided to jump on the bandwagon. I should have known better than to trust you. I can't believe how stupid I was."

"You know what? I'll bet that the stuff is too powerful, Christina. You probably need to dilute it or something. Yeah, that's it, I'll bet. I'll bet you just have to dilute it."

"Or maybe I'll just need to cut off my hand, Uncle Vinnie."

"Don't be absurd."

"I can't talk to you right now, Uncle Vinnie. I've got to see what I can do with this stuff before it winds up rotting away my flesh. I'll talk to you later."

And with that, she hung up on him and went into the bathroom to soak her hand in the sink.

18
CATCHING UP
TO SNAKE

*B*y the time she was ready for bed, Christina had managed to get her hand to the point where it was no longer itching her although her skin was still red and sore from where the face crème had been. That was the last time that she was going to trust Uncle Vinnie, she decided. When was she going to learn that the man wasn't ever going to do the right thing?

She was still thinking about Uncle Vinnie when she dozed off and found herself back in The Jungle. She saw Bird sitting on a tree branch, as if waiting for her, and Christina smiled. "Hello, Bird."

"Hello, Christina," Bird trilled, landing on her shoulder.

Christina started to walk down the path, and she recognized it as the one that led to the clearing where Snake was always at work. She wasn't surprised to find Snake there along with Warthog. Nearby, Cougar seemed to be taking an afternoon nap, but Christina was focused on Snake. At the moment, he was weaving back and forth, speaking in a plaintive tone to Warthog, "But you have to have the right ingredients in order to fly, Warthog. Don't you want to fly?"

Warthog shook his head. "No."

"Why not? Why don't you want to be the first flying warthog? Think of it, you soaring through the clouds, everyone watching you and cheering?"

Christina looked at Bird. "Why doesn't Snake just give up?" she asked.

Bird sighed. "Snake is persistent, and while that can be an admirable trait for a sales animal, he never has a good product. He thinks that he can keep on picking and picking and picking at someone until they just give up and then sells them something of little or no value."

"It doesn't sound like Warthog is going to give-in this time though."

Bird chuckled. "No, it doesn't. And that means that Snake is going to have to go out there and find someone else that he can trick."

"When will he learn that's not the way to do things?"

"With Snake, there's no telling. It's possible that he's never going to learn."

At that moment, Snake came slithering over to them. He looked at Christina for a moment then turned his attention to Bird. "Hey, Bird, don't you ever get tired of flying around in the sky all the time? Don't you ever wish that you could just take it easy and try something else?"

"Like what, Snake?" Bird asked.

"I was thinking that you might want to be in the water once in a while. You could be under the water, swimming around with fishes, and they'd all be looking at you and thinking, 'That's Bird, but he's with us fishes. He's truly the greatest bird in the whole world.' That's what they'd be thinking, Bird."

"I don't want to be in the water, Snake. I like flying. It's what I do—because Bird is who I am."

Snake looked at Christina. "What about you, Girl? Isn't there something that you want that you can't have? I can give it to you, you know. You ask anyone."

"I have a feeling if I ask anyone about you, Snake, I'm not going to hear very many good things."

"Go on with you. Anyone who says bad things about Snake is jealous of Snake, that's all. They know that Snake can do anything, and they're jealous."

Christina laughed. "That's okay. I think I'm fine with what I have right now."

Snake shook his head. "Okay with you, then. But don't come running to Snake when you need something because I'll be with someone else by then." And with that, he slithered away.

"Like I said, Snake might never learn," Bird said, and there was sadness in her voice.

MAKING THE
CUSTOMER HAPPY

*B*y the time that Christina made it to class, the effects of the crème had finally begun to wear off. There was still a slight itchiness to her skin, but it was nothing that she couldn't live with. On the other hand, she was upset that she even had to think about "living with" the effects of Uncle Vinnie's crème. That just wasn't right.

Taking her seat, she saw that Professor Krenkle had put something on the board: "A satisfied customer might never tell anyone about how wonderful your service is, but a dissatisfied customer will tell everyone." Glancing over at Peterson, she saw the student shake his head as if amazed at the naïveté of the sentiment.

Professor Krenkle came to the front of the class and stood there for a moment, looking out at their faces. There was a slight smile on his lips, and he said, "I know that some of you are thinking that the sort of material I cover is old-fashioned and out-dated and wonder why a professor of new thought teaches 'old stuff.' I can assure you that what you learn here is going to be useful in every aspect of your sales careers. In fact, I might go so far as to tell you that it's going to be useful in just about every aspect of your lives, and if it works, it doesn't matter if it's old school or new."

Peterson raised his hand.

"Yes, Mr. Peterson?"

"I know that you're trying to help us out, Professor, but I think you need to be a little more in-step with what's out there. Sure, in the old days, it probably made good sense to try to keep every customer happy, but we're in an age where that's impossible. There are too many customers out there for anyone to make them all happy."

The professor chuckled. "Is that actually what you think, Mr. Peterson?"

"Yes, sir."

"Well, I hate to be the one to break this to you, but you're wrong. In today's society, it's more important than ever to make sure that your customers are happy. Do you want to know why that is?"

The student rolled his eyes. "Do tell," he said, and there were some chuckles that were quickly silenced.

"We live in an electronic age, and if you provide someone with an inferior product, it's no longer a case of them telling their friends and families about what you've done. It goes beyond that. There are websites now that will allow people to post any dissatisfaction they might have, and that means that while there was a time when you might only alienate two or three people at a time, we're now living in an age where you can get a lot more than that upset at you."

"But how can you make everyone happy?"

The old man shook his head. "You can't—but there are things that you can do to lessen the likelihood of dissatisfied customers. You can listen to your customers and find out what their needs are. You can deal with them honestly and forthrightly. You can make sure that the product you're providing meets whatever rigid standards you've set up."

"What about people who are never going to be happy, though?"

Professor Krenkle shook his head. "Those are the ones that you just have to let go, I'm afraid. There are always going to be people out there who simply can't find their way to happiness, no matter what you do."

Christina raised her hand. "Professor Krenkle, when do you know when a customer is going to be just too difficult?"

"Good question, Christina. I've found that when I've accommodated them for the third or fourth time and they still aren't satisfied, I have to let them go. I always do it in as polite a manner as possible, and simply make a note that they're not someone that I'm ever going to please."

She nodded. "Thank you."

The professor looked out over the class. "Remember, though, the customers who you simply cannot please are

few and far between. For the most part, you'll be able to make everyone happy, as long as you provide them with good service and treat them fairly and with respect. Always treat your customers the way you want to be treated, and you usually can't go wrong."

UNCLE VINNIE HAS YET ANOTHER PRODUCT

When Christina came home from school, she found Uncle Vinnie waiting for her. For a moment, she couldn't believe that he was actually there, but he held up his hands in mock surrender and said, "Hold on! Before you ask me to get out of here, let me tell you why I've come here."

She waited, standing there with arms folded, not willing to let herself get tricked again.

Uncle Vinnie took out a small bottle and held it up. "Do you know what's in here?"

"I'm afraid to ask."

He gave her a hurt look. "Don't be that way. In this vial, you're going to find that I've managed to capture the one thing that you've always wanted."

"What's that—a way to keep you from involving me in any more of your schemes?"

"This is a new kind of shampoo that is designed to make your hair thick and luxurious, and it's hard to get your hands on too. I got a sample, and I knew that I had to let you try it."

Christina regarded him with wary eyes. "Is this something that I'm supposed to be testing or something?"

He gave her a hurt look. "I can't believe that you even asked me that."

"Forgive me for being cynical, but the face crème that you gave me nearly ate through my skin."

"This is totally on the level. I've seen this stuff in action, and I'm telling you, right now, you're not going to believe what it can do. When you're done with it, you're going to thank me and never doubt me again."

Christina took the sample and allowed herself a slight smile. "If it's as good as you say, I'll be the first to apologize, Uncle Vinnie."

"I'll be waiting for your phone call."

LEARNING FROM THE PAST

Christina sat in the back of the classroom, a baseball cap pulled low over her head. She couldn't believe what had happened, and she prayed that she could get through the day without being humiliated by someone noticing what had happened.

Professor Krenkle stepped in front of the class and said, "Today, we're not going to talk about sales. Instead, we're going to talk about business because no matter what you're selling, and no matter whom you're selling it for—your own company or the company you work for—you are in business.

"Up to this point we've been talking mainly about making sure your customer believes in you, that you offer good customer service, and that you have a product that is worthwhile. However, sales require an enormous amount of work outside of the actual selling situation, an aspect of operating a successful business that many people don't consider.

"Remember the first lesson I taught you about delegating? Well there's more than one way to delegate all that you must do to be a successful salesperson. You see in most cases, you're going to have to deal with people outside of your organization whether it is with goods or from services. That being the case, you need to understand that one important aspect of a successful business is choosing the right vendors to work with.

"Now, who can tell me what the most important aspect of working with a good vendor might be?"

Peterson raised his hand.

"Yes, Mr. Peterson?"

"You need to find someone who can give you the best price," the student said.

Krenkle shook his head. "Actually, nothing could be further from the truth. When it comes to dealing with businesses, it's not always in your best interest to try to save money. Often, that can lead to inferior work or services."

A young girl raised her hand.

"Yes?"

"How do you know which are the best people to deal with?" she asked.

"Ideally, it should be someone that you know personally. After that, you need to deal with someone who has credentials that can be checked out. Don't be afraid to ask for references. The important thing is that you make sure that you're being dealt with fairly and honestly."

Peterson raised his hand again.

"Yes, Mr. Peterson?"

"I think it's stupid to pay more for work that someone else can do cheaper."

"In other words, you think that the smart business move would be to save a few pennies here and there?"

"Absolutely. When you take care of the small details, the big details take care of themselves," the student said.

Professor Krenkle laughed. "And, do you think it would be worth it to save some money in the immediate future and then to lose a lot of money down the road?"

"Well, no, but—"

"That's what would happen if you went with someone solely on the basis of what they're costing you. Who can tell me an important element in picking the right business to deal with?"

A bearded young man in the first row raised his hand. "Yes, Mr. Thorne?"

"Find out their track record?" he asked, hesitantly.

The professor nodded. "Yes, indeed. Do you want to know something that is absolutely amazing about businesses with faulty track records? In many cases, someone will use a business that failed to meet their expectations, but when the time comes to use that business again, the customer will actually go back a second time." Christina saw him looking at her, and she felt as if he were seeing right into her.

"Most of us want to believe the best in others, but there comes a time when we have to realize if we've been burned by a business, it's ridiculous to go back to them for another chance to ruin things," the old man said, and pointed at Christina. "Christina, I'm sure that it's a trick of the lighting, but please tell me that I'm imagining the fact that it looks like you have green hair."

Everyone turned around and looked at her. Christina, face red with embarrassment, took off the baseball cap. Everyone stared at her green hair. "My uncle," she explained, "gave me a shampoo that was supposed to be the greatest shampoo in the world, but unfortunately it turned my hair green."

"Yes, it did."

"And the thing is I should have known better. My uncle gave me a face crème that burned my skin, so why in the world would I have thought that this shampoo would have been worthwhile?"

Professor Krenkle nodded. "In a way, you're like the great many people I just mentioned, Christina. You want to believe the best in people, and there's nothing wrong with that. In fact, there are going to be times when you're in business that things are going to come up that are out of your control and you're not going to be able to please your customer. The good news, though, is that most people will give you a second chance. But no matter if you are a customer or a business owner, after you've given someone a second chance, it's best to walk away—or else, there's no telling what might happen to your hair next."

THE IMPORTANCE OF A GIFT

*T*he next time that Christina dreamt of The Jungle, she found herself sitting by a gently rolling river with Bird resting on a nearby bush. Raccoon was a short distance away, and Christina was going over to talk to him when Warthog entered the clearing.

It was obvious that Warthog was feeling very bad. His head was down, and he moved slowly as if his entire world had fallen apart. Thinking about how much Warthog had wanted to fly, Christina understood how he felt, and her heart went out to him. "Poor Warthog," she said to Bird.

Bird nodded. "Poor Warthog is right. Snake took advantage of him, and that wasn't right. Snake knew that Warthog wanted to fly more than anything, and he never should have done that."

Warthog went to sit by the river, and let out a loud sigh. A few moments later, Raccoon came over to him. "What's wrong, Warthog?"

"I can't fly," he said.

Raccoon stared at him. "Well, of course you can't fly. You're a warthog. Warthogs don't fly."

"Snake sold me some stuff that was supposed to make me fly," Warthog said. "He lied to me."

"Snake does that."

"How could he do that?"

Raccoon shrugged. "He's Snake. He doesn't see that he's doing wrong because he thinks that if someone is silly enough to trust him, that's their own fault."

"That's not right."

"No, it's not, but there are a lot of animals out there like Snake. They tell themselves that it's no big deal if they take advantage of other animals. They also think it's not their job to make sure that animals in general don't take advantage of other animals, but that's wrong. It's not good to be dishonest with anyone."

Warthog sighed again. "I just wanted to fly."

Raccoon looked at him for a moment, then reached into his pocket and took out a beautiful blue stone. It was the color of a magnificent spring day, and Warthog's eyes widened when he saw it.

"That's beautiful, Raccoon."

"Yes, it is. It's a special stone, you know."

Warthog watched him carefully. "It's not magic, is it?"

Raccoon laughed, shaking his head. "No, it's not magic."

"That's good because Snake tried to sell me magic, and there's no such thing."

"This is just special because there have been times when I've felt depressed and blue, Warthog, but I just look at this stone, and it makes me think of the sky. I close my eyes, and I imagine what it would be like to fly. Then, I always feel better."

Warthog stared at Raccoon. "But you're not really flying."

"Of course not—Raccoons can't fly."

"But—" Warthog began, then stopped. "Oh, wait a minute. I see what you're saying. You're saying that Warthogs can't fly, either."

"No, they can't."

"But we can dream about flying, and when we stop dreaming about it, we still have this beautiful stone."

"Yes."

Warthog frowned, his eyes narrowed. "How much is this going to cost me?" he asked.

Raccoon shook his head. "No money, Warthog. It's a gift from me to you."

"Why?"

"Because I want you to have it. I want you to know that not everyone who wants to sell you something is a bad person. Maybe the next time that you need something, you'll come to see me instead of Snake."

Warthog nodded. "I will, Raccoon. I definitely will."

Christina watched as Warthog walked away, his blue stone held tightly in his mouth and was amazed at how quickly he became happy and upbeat. Bird whistled out a little laugh. "That Raccoon," Bird said, "knows how to be a great salesman, that's for sure."

23
THINKING OUTSIDE THE BOX

When Christina went to class the next day, Professor Krenkle stood in front of the class and said, "It's important that all of you understand the concept of thinking outside the box. Too many times, we're trapped in ways of thinking that are familiar and safe, but in today's new marketplace, that's not the way to go. More than ever, you've got people out there who are doing their best to get every bit of business out there, and it's going to be your job to find a way to carve your own niche."

Peterson raised his hand—naturally.

The professor nodded at him.

"Yes, Mr. Peterson?"

"What about advertising, Professor Krenkle?"

"What kind of advertising?"

"A media blitz," Peterson said. "You know. You go with print and television and Internet and an e-mail campaign and—"

Professor Krenkle held up a hand. "Are you independently wealthy, Mr. Peterson?"

"No, sir."

"Then, how do you propose to pay for this media blitz of yours?"

Peterson frowned. "I guess with whatever start-up money I have."

"The kind of advertising that you're talking about is going to use up all of your start-up money, Mr. Peterson."

"Well, then, I guess I'd think about taking out a loan. Once you get them hooked, it'll be easy to sell them whatever it is that you're selling."

"That's no longer the case, I'm afraid. The only way that you're going to maintain a strong sales presence is to make sure that you've given your customers exactly what they're looking for. You also need to show your customers that you are creative and innovate and are thinking of new ways to serve them all the time."

Peterson shook his head. "Professor Krenkle, I think you're still dealing with an old-fashioned model here. Sure, there was a time when it was important to be all the way down-the-line and by-the-book, but those days are past. There are lots of companies out there that are cutting corners and aren't being totally honest."

The old man nodded. "Yes, there are."

"So, what's wrong with that?"

"Nothing—but they'll be gone in six months or less. I've seen it time after time. Yes, a company might start off with a big splash, but if they're not honest or they don't have a decent product to back up all the buzz, the 'bang' quickly dries up, and the next thing you know, they're gone without a trace."

"But, if you get enough people right away, you can afford to lose a certain percentage."

"Wrong. In business, losing one customer is one customer too many. Yes, there are going to be some customers that you simply can't satisfy, but they are the minority. So, can anyone tell me a way they have of attracting interest in whatever it is that they're selling?"

Christina raised her hand. "I have an idea, Professor Krenkle."

"What is it?"

"What about offering some sort of free gift?"

Peterson snorted. "Yeah, right. Like giving something away is going to make you money."

The professor ignored him. "What kind of free gift?"

"I'm not sure. I guess it depends on the product. But, whatever it is, it should be useful. I've gone to places and gotten a free gift that was absolutely worthless, and that made me just want to stay away from the company. If you're going to give something away, make it something that's useful."

Professor Krenkle nodded. "You're absolutely right. I once bought some coffee from a company on the Internet, and they gave me a free coffeemaker, provided that I buy one pound of their coffee beans. I did so and I'm still using the coffeemaker to this day—and I'm still buying my coffee from the company."

A tall man raised his hand. "I know what you're talking about. I went into this one used bookstore, and the owner was giving away a free book with every purchase. We could choose what we wanted from a box of books he had set aside, and they were good books, too. I've been getting all of my used books from that store since."

The professor nodded, smiling broadly. "When you offer a free gift to a potential customer, you are well on your way to getting a customer for life. The important thing, however, is to make sure that you're actually giving something away that's worthwhile, not something that's useless and inefficient."

THE THREE TYPES OF CONFIDENCE

*T*he next day in class, Professor Krenkle had written on the board: "The Three Types of Confidence," and when everyone was seated, he pointed towards what he had written.

"Now, then," he said, "as individuals who are going to attempt to be great salespersons, you're going to need to understand the importance of confidence. Confidence in yourself is obvious and is a very important part of selling a product. However, you also need to have two other kinds of confidence. Who can tell me what they are?"

Christina thought for a moment and then raised her hand.

"Yes, Christina?"

"I think you need to have confidence in the product," she suggested.

Professor Krenkle nodded. "Precisely. You need to have confidence in what you're selling. If you don't have that, you need to walk away from that product right away, because you're not going to be successful at what you're selling. I don't care how good a salesperson you are, you are not going to be able to convince people to buy what you're selling if you don't believe in it.

"Now, who can tell me what other kind of confidence is important?"

Peterson raised his hand.

"Yes, Mr. Peterson?"

"You need confidence in whatever system you're using to sell. You need to focus on the sales plan and make sure that you stick to it, no matter what. When you start to lose confidence in your system, you're going to fail."

The professor shook his head, "that's not what I was looking for, I'm afraid."

Peterson rolled his eyes. "Why am I not surprised?"

A heavyset student with glasses in the back row raised his hand, looking very nervous. "Yes, Mr. Adams? I believe this is the first time that you've volunteered to answer a question. I'm glad to see that you're participating."

The student nervously licked his lips. "Uh…I was wondering if…if you needed to have confidence in the customer."

The old man beamed with delight. "Yes! You need to have confidence that your customer is going to want to buy the product that you're selling *and* that your customer is bright enough to see the benefits of what you're selling."

Peterson snorted.

"Did you have something that you wanted to say, Mr. Peterson?"

"I was just thinking that I've dealt with a lot of people who I don't have enough confidence in to tie their own shoes," he said.

"I might suggest that you're going to have a hard time selling to those people, Mr. Peterson."

"Professor, do you understand how hard it is in today's marketplace to do what you're telling us to do? I mean, no offense, but if we all followed your suggestions, we'd wind up getting our butts kicked by the competition."

The old man shook his head. "No, you wouldn't. Yes, there might be a period when others are doing better than you by using devious methods, but in the long run, those who don't do right by the customer are going to fail. It's as simple as that. Now, before you go, I want you to know that I have a very important announcement to make tomorrow, so be prepared for something very exciting."

UNCLE VINNIE
HAS AN OFFER

After class, Christina went home and Uncle Vinnie was waiting outside her apartment. For a moment, Christina thought that she'd try to make a quick escape before he spotted her, but he saw her and came towards her with a serious expression on his face.

"Uncle Vinnie, I really don't want to say anything to you," she said, opening her door.

He followed her into the apartment. "I want to talk to you."

"Seriously. I have nothing that I want to say to you."

Her uncle gave her a sad hangdog expression. "This is something that I think you're really going to like."

"I'm not interested."

"I want to give you some money to start your own business."

Christina stopped and gave him a long expression. "What are you trying to pull, Uncle Vinnie?"

"I'm just thinking that I probably have been working the wrong angle with you. I'm thinking that I've made a serious mistake about what I was doing, and I want to fix it."

"What's the angle?"

He gave her an innocent look. "What do you mean?"

"Uncle Vinnie, let's be honest here. You're always scamming me. What makes you think that I'm falling for this foolishness?"

"I'm totally on the level here. Look, you're trying to run your own business, right? Well, I want to help you. I want to give you some money to start your own business."

"And what's the catch?"

Again, he shook his head. "No catch."

Christina's features soften. "Well, I have to admit, that's a great gift. I know that I have what it takes to really be a great salesperson, but I wasn't sure if I was going to be able to get the money that I need to start my own art business. I've always dreamed about owning my own gallery."

"Now you don't have to worry."

She gave him a warm smile. "Thank you."

"And, the best part is, we'll be working together."

"What?"

Uncle Vinnie gave her a wink. "It's perfect. You'll be the salesperson, and I'll be the one who—"

"Get out," Christina said.

"What?"

"You heard me. Get out. I don't want to discuss this any longer. I'm not going to take any money from you."

"But how do you think you're going to get the money that you need?" he asked.

Christina shrugged. "I don't know," she finally said, "but I won't do it going into business with you. If I'm going to succeed, I'm going to do it my way—and I'm going to do it the honest way. Period."

He shook his head. "You don't know what a serious mistake you're making," he said and left the apartment.

Christina shook her head. "When will I ever learn?" she muttered.

THE CHALLENGE

*T*he following day, Christina was still trying to figure out how she was going to raise the money to get a good start with her business, but she pushed those thoughts away when she arrived at Professor Krenkle's class.

"Now then class, I'm pleased to tell you that you appear to be among the brightest students that it's ever been my pleasure to teach, and that's why I've arranged for something special. I know that all of you are interested in starting your own businesses, and I've arranged with a friend of mine who is interested in helping out new businesses to give you an incentive to put you on the right track.

"Each of you will be given samples of a new hand lotion that I want you to give out to people."

Christina raised her hand. "What kind of hand lotion is this, Professor Krenkle?"

The old man laughed. "I can assure you that it's fine, Christina."

"Just checking."

Peterson raised his hand.

"Yes, Mr. Peterson?"

"You want us to sell it, right?"

"No. I want you to give it away."

"I don't get it. That's going to be easy."

"It certainly should be, assuming that you've paid attention in class. However, there's more to it than just giving away the sample. I also want you to get names and phone numbers from your prospects as well as sign them up for future products."

Peterson grinned. "Piece of cake."

"At the end of the day, the student who has achieved the best success with building up a customer base will be given the opportunity to have my friend arrange to invest in their start-up company. How does that sound?"

Christina could barely contain her excitement. This was better than she had imagined. If she was able to beat Peterson, she'd be able to get her business off the ground, and she'd be on her way to achieving her dream.

The problem was she didn't know if her style of selling was going to be good enough to fight the tactics she was sure Peterson was going to use. There was only one way to find out. "Let the selling begin," she said, under her breath.

She hoped that she'd be able to pull this off.

THE CHALLENGE

Christina had been so nervous she'd been unable to sleep very well. There had been brief moments of dreams—Snake, Warthog, Raccoon, and Bird were all there—but when she woke up, she was tired and convinced that there was no way this was going to end well.

"Who am I kidding?" she asked herself, looking in the mirror. "This isn't going to work for me. Peterson has all the angles. He's going to beat me." But, if there was one thing that Christina had learned early on in her life, it was that the only way possible for someone to succeed was to actually go out and make the attempt. Sure, she might fail—but she also knew that the only sure-fire way to make sure that you didn't succeed was to make sure that you didn't try at all.

When she got to the mall, everyone waited with a sense of excitement. Peterson glanced over at her and smirked, and for a moment Christina actually thought briefly about just walking away from this and forgetting the whole thing. Instead, she walked confidently over to Professor Krenkle who handed her a small plastic bag that had hand lotion samples in it. She decided she was going to make this a positive experience, no matter what.

The professor gave her a warm smile. "Here you are, Christina. I'm sure you're going to do fine."

"I know I will," she said.

The professor addressed the class. "All right, then. You know what to do. Go on out there, give away your samples, and build up a customer base. Now, go."

The students scattered, but Christina paused for a moment, thinking things through. She saw that several of the students were gathered near the east entrance of the mall—the most popular area. But, with three students for every person who walked in, the odds were there was going to be too much competition in that area.

She went to the north entrance. That entrance had fewer people passing through it, but there were no other students around. Christina quickly discovered that giving away samples was harder than she thought. Several people just walked right past her without even glancing at her, and when she tried to give the sample to others, they waved her away with their hand.

She wondered how Peterson was doing. Eventually, though, she was able to give away a couple of samples and get some contact information. Her confidence was building when she noticed an old woman standing off to one side, looking confused. Christina went over to her. "Is everything all right, ma'am?"

The woman turned to her with worried eyes. "I seem to have misplaced my grandson, I'm afraid. He was right here next to me, and the next thing I knew, I couldn't find him."

The poor old woman looked as if she were about to burst into tears, and Christina said, "Don't worry. I'll help you find him."

"Thank you so much, dear. That would be wonderful."

There was a part of Christina that knew she was making a mistake here, that she should be working on getting her samples sold, but she also knew that the old woman was very upset and worried. Christina couldn't imagine going on about her business while the woman was in trouble.

So for the next hour, Christina and the old woman went through the mall, looking carefully for the woman's grandson. Christina knew that with each passing moment she was achieving less and less of her goal, but she couldn't help herself. She had to do the right thing.

Eventually, she was actually able to find the missing grandson who turned out to be a very handsome young man about Christina's age. He had the nicest blue eyes she'd ever seen, and when her hugged his grandmother in obvious relief, Christina knew that she'd done the right thing.

"Thank you so much," he told Christina. "You didn't have to do that. I'm Andrew, by the way." He extended his hand, and she took it.

"I'm Christina, and it was nothing. I saw she was having some problems, and I wanted to make sure I helped her out."

"You did a wonderful thing here. I'm going to make sure that I don't forget that."

"It was nothing," Christina said, and glanced at her watch. "I've got to go—I'm in the middle of something."

He looked somewhat disappointed. "Well, it was definitely nice meeting you," he said.

Christina rushed to the other end of the mall where Professor Krenkle waited, along with Peterson, who had a smug expression on his face.

"Look who finally showed up," Peterson said, with a sneer. "Glad to see you could make it."

Professor Krenkle gave her a long look. "Is everything all right, Christina?"

She sighed. "I guess so. I didn't get rid of all my samples, though. I was helping someone out."

Peterson laughed. "Figures. That's what happens when you try to be Miss Goody-Two-Shoes in the business world. You lose every time."

The professor gave her a solemn look. "I'm sorry, Christina, but it does look like you've lost the challenge."

She only nodded, tears in her eyes, for she didn't trust herself to speak. "I understand," she finally said.

At that moment, a voice behind her said, "Professor Krenkle?"

Christina was startled at how familiar the voice sounded, and she turned around. Andrew and his grand-

mother were standing there. Professor Krenkle beamed when he saw the young man and he gave him an affectionate handshake. "Andrew Keller—my best and most promising student. How are you?"

"Doing well, professor. My fifth company just took off like gangbusters, and I'm working on a revenue-sharing deal with Apple that is going to be very rewarding," he said, then noticed Christina. "We meet again."

Professor Krenkle raised his eyebrows.

"You two know each other?"

"Actually, we just met," Andrew said. "This lovely young woman helped out my grandmother, and I was just wondering how in the world I could thank her for the kindness she extended to a total stranger."

"Christina is one of my students, Andrew—and one of the best I've got. We were having a competition, but it doesn't look like she managed to win this one."

Andrew looked at her carefully and Christina stared into his eyes, watching as a slight smile appeared on his lips. "You helped my grandmother when you could have been winning your competition?" he asked.

Christina felt her face heat up. "Uh—I guess so."

"I'm impressed. Professor Krenkle, you always manage to find the best students out there," he said and took out a business card. "Tell you what Christina. I want to get Grandma home. She's had a rough morning. But I want

you to call me this afternoon so that I can talk about investment opportunities with you."

She gave him a blank look. "Investment opportunities?"

He nodded. "Definitely. I'm always looking for new businesses to invest in, and I've got a feeling that I can't go wrong with someone like you. Call me." And with that, he and his grandmother left. Christina stared at the card in her hand, her mouth open.

Peterson's mouth was also hanging open. "That was Andrew Keller," he said, stunned. "He's one of the richest men in the country."

Professor Krenkle nodded. "Yes, he is."

"And—" he turned to stare at Christina "—he wants to invest with you."

Christina looked at him with a stunned expression. "I guess so."

"But, I'm the one who won the competition, so I should be the one to get this opportunity."

Professor Krenkle shook his head. "Of course not. You won the competition, so you'll be getting some start-up funding from my friend. Christina here lost the competition but gained an invaluable contact in the business world."

"But....but...."

The professor held up one hand. "You see, Mr. Peterson, you insist upon treating business as if you're in some kind of jungle, with every man for himself. But, we're not living in a jungle. We're living in a world filled with people who deserve the best that you have to give them—even if it means losing a sale—or a competition.

"Many people think selling is like surviving in a jungle. They think it's hard, dirty, and dangerous work. I find that it is not a jungle at all, and so do many others who have successful businesses. If you truly care about your customers, if you're selling them a product that you believe will add value to their lives, then you don't have to feel that your customers are against you. But, Mister Peterson, if you think it is a jungle, then you'll struggle and find it difficult to succeed. If you hold the attitude that your work serves others, and you sell what you are excited about, then you'll find 'the jungle' is really more like a loving, tame pet."

Christina stared at the card in her hand and knew that she was well on her way to achieving the success she'd wanted for so long.

WHAT YOU NEED TO LEARN IN ORDER TO BE SUCCESSFUL IN SALES

Tips and tactics used by successful salespersons throughout the business world that have been shown to be virtually "bulletproof."

THE IMPORTANCE OF SELLING YOURSELF

One of the most important lessons that you need to understand about being a successful salesperson is that you are the most valuable part of the sales equation. Forget whatever you've heard about having to have a fantastic product that will sell itself.

The days of items selling themselves are long gone.

One of the best examples of a successful salesperson is none other than Steve Jobs of Apple, Incorporated. At one time, Apple was trailing far behind Microsoft in terms of computer sales and their stock price wasn't where the investors wanted it to be.

Steve Jobs set about selling people on Apple. First, however, he sold them on himself. He undertook a campaign designed entirely on his own efforts to make Apple into the company that the consumers wanted. He made sure that whenever the name Apple came up, people also thought of Steve Jobs.

In relatively no time at all, Apple became one of the top industry leaders in terms of computing, and to this

day, the loyalty among Apple consumers is unlike any-thing else encountered.

Why?

Steve Jobs made sure that people trusted him and his product, and once he accomplished that, the sky was liter-ally the limit. You can achieve the same thing.

HOW TO SELL YOURSELF

*H*aving discussed how important it is to sell yourself, we need to take a look at just how it is that you'll be able to accomplish that.

First of all, you need to make sure that your potential customers have trust in you. This means that you have to be square and upfront in all of your dealings with all of your customers. Because of the way the Internet works, a bad reputation can move quickly across the country, and just because someone is separated by distance doesn't mean that they can't affect your future business dealings.

Selling yourself doesn't mean building yourself up dishonestly. What it means is that you deliver the goods that you say you're going to deliver and that you honor any commitments you make to your potential customers.

One shining example of this can be found with the people who came out with the Saturn car. When they first started, their reputation was sterling. People talked about having had problems with their Saturns and having dealers drive two hundred miles to make things right. Before

long, Saturn had a really terrific reputation, and that reputation is continuing to this day.

Naturally, there are times when you simply won't be able to accommodate a customer, and the best that you can do under those circumstances is to put forth a sincere effort and know that you did your best. If you always conduct business with an attitude of serving others, and you do what you reasonably can to make the customer happy, you will do fine. However, you do have to hold to standards and boundaries, and if a customer is violating them, it is time to let them go.

LISTEN TO YOUR CUSTOMER

*I*f there's one tactic that successful salespersons all over the world have in common, it's the fact that they've managed to perfect listening to their potential customers.

Nothing is more important to a customer than knowing that they are being listened to. The way this works is that when you are dealing with the customer, you completely forget about whatever it is that you're trying to sell.

Put it out of your mind.

Instead, concentrate on what the customer is talking about and what the customer is looking for. Period. Don't worry about how you can best tailor the needs of the customer to what you're currently selling. That's not important. The customer is going to know if you're trying to sell them something they're not looking for, and they're going to walk away from you.

Now, what if you don't have what the customer is looking for? First, you can tell them that you're not carrying that particular item, and then you can suggest possible alternatives.

Recently, I had occasion to go into a mattress store, looking for a particular kind of pillow that is supposed to increase oxygen flow during the night. It is reported to be very efficient and practical. However, when I arrived, the store was entirely sold out of them.

I spoke to the salesperson for a few minutes, and when he found out that I also had trouble getting to sleep, he showed me a small electronic device that was designed to help people get to sleep faster and to enter a deeper sleep. I decided to give it a try, and to my great delight, I found out that it worked.

Had the salesperson not listened to what I was looking for and had he not been honest with me that they were out of the pillows, I would have left and that would have been the end of it. By listening to me, by getting to what I needed, however, he was able to give me something that worked, and two days later, when the pillow in question was back in stock, he called me and I bought the pillow as well.

Remember—listen to your customer.

SELL QUALITY PRODUCTS

*J*ust as important as it is to sell a customer on yourself, you also need to be able to show them that you're selling quality products. After all, if you're selling something that's useless, what's the point of even working hard at being a good salesman? One of the most important aspects of good salesmanship is making sure that you do right by the customer, and you're not going to be able to do that if you're selling something that you know is an inferior product.

This doesn't mean that you have to only sell items that are expensive and top-of- the-line. After all, a lot of people out there are looking for things that are well-made and affordable. The salesperson who specializes in selling items that meet those criteria is a salesperson who is going to be extremely successful at what he or she does.

Now, more than ever, people are finding that their money isn't going nearly as far as it once did, and they are looking to find value. A good salesperson is someone who is able to show a customer the value in the items that they are selling.

For example, what if you are selling something that costs more than an item that looks similar? Your potential customer is going to come over to you and say, "Why the heck should I spend more money on your product when I can get something similar for half that price?"

At that point, you'll want to point out why your item has more value than the competition. "This item costs less," you might explain, "but the manufacturing behind it isn't nearly as good as what we're selling. If you pull up the reviews on the Internet, for example, you'll see the competition's product doesn't perform nearly as well—and has a higher failure rate than ours. We want to make sure that our customers have a pleasant experience when they use this product, which is why we go out of our way to make sure that we only sell an item that has value."

Once you're able to show—in a totally honest and forthright way—why the products that you're selling are better than those of a competitor, you'll be well on your way to building up a loyal customer base.

CONTACT INFORMATION

A successful salesperson maintains contact with the customer, even after the sale. This one little aspect, so often neglected, is what can turn a one-time customer into someone who is a loyal customer for life.

When we buy something, we don't want to think that our interaction with the salesperson is just about the sale. Sure, that might actually be the way that it is, but that's not what we want to think. Instead, we want to think that a genuine connection was made. A follow-up call is all about making that connection last.

Many of us have had the experience of having a salesperson call when we've been sitting on the fence about buying something, a new car, a house, etc. But, how many of us have ever had a follow-up call after we've purchased the item? Probably not as many as you would think. But the fact is that follow-up call should be the most important one you make because it lets the customer know that the experience was not about you making the sale but about him or her being happy with what they purchased.

It's all about building a relationship between the salesperson and the customer, and when you've got that kind of connection built up, you'll accomplish two things. First, you'll have someone who is going to be a part of your customer base for a long time. Second, they will, more often than not, give you a favorable build-up to friends and family.

In many cases, I've seen successful salespersons build up such a strong satisfied customer base that it carried over into online forums—and their business doubled and tripled when *that* happened. So, after the sale is made, don't forget to touch base with the customer to make sure that their buying experience was what they had hoped it would be, and to find out if there is any way that you can improve on what you've already done.

When you let them know they are valued, your customers will make a point of doing business with you in the future.

THE POWER OF A POSITIVE ATTITUDE

One of the best ways to be a successful salesperson is to maintain a positive attitude, and yet this seemingly obvious piece of information escapes the notice of a great many people involved with sales.

You would think that most people would understand the importance of a genuinely positive attitude, but the truth is most salespersons don't grasp the concept. They know that it's important to "appear" to be positive, but in fact, it's more important to actually *be* positive. The customer can sense when someone is being false or phony, and nothing is a bigger turn-off than dealing with someone who is smiling but who you know isn't being genuine.

"But, what if I'm in a bad mood?" you might ask.

Simple. Get out of it.

You have the power to change your thoughts and emotions, after all. You can choose to be in a foul mood and you can choose to be in a good mood. Why would you want to waste time and energy being in a bad mood

when you can just as easily walk away from it and remain in a good mood?

You're the master of your emotions, so before you even head to work in the morning, what you need to do is take a few moments to just compose yourself, put yourself in the right state of mind, and then go ahead and get yourself into a good mood. Reflect on the many good things that you have going on in your life, and don't worry about or dwell on the negative aspects.

The more positive you are, the more positive your customers will be, *and* they'll want to be around you and do business with you.

CONCLUSION

*I*n today's competitive world, it's harder than ever to really make it as a successful salesperson, to really generate the kind of money that many of us are looking for.

That's the bad news.

The good news, however, is that more and more people are getting dissatisfied with bad salespersons, and they are actively looking for new avenues to service their needs. There are more and more companies out there to choose from, and it is easy to find places to do business with by simply going online. This means that you've got a better chance to make an impression and to succeed where others are failing. What's important is that you do right by the customer.

It's not about the sale. It never has been. The one constant in sales is that it is always and has always been about the customer-salesperson experience. Whether you're actually meeting someone in a brick-and-mortar store or whether you're dealing with someone online, the important thing is that you find a way to connect to them on a genuine level. You do what it takes to make sure that

they're satisfied, and you even allow them to walk away when they're not interested in what you're selling.

Those are the tactics that the most successful salespersons use. It is the essence of sell without selling, and it's actually been around for decades without being improved upon. For you see, there's a difference between "methods" and "tactics." Selling methods, the avenues by which we sell, have changed somewhat because of new technologies such as the Internet. But the tactics, the *ways* we sell, are still the same. And if some may call these tactics "old-fashioned" so be it. If something works, why change it? Sure, there are going to be times when you're stressed out, when things aren't going as well as you might like, but as long as you keep in mind all of the sell-without-selling lessons that you've been taught, you'll definitely come out ahead. You will be the success that you so richly deserve.

Good luck and have fun.

ABOUT THE AUTHOR

Dr. Terri Levine, The Guru of Coaching®, is a Master Certified Coach, bestselling author, and a sales-coaching and training expert. She created the world renowned "Selling-Without-Selling" program (http://www.TerriLevine.com/packages.html#selling) that has been delivered to corporations worldwide.

Terri has an impressive track record using her sell-without-selling approach and was number one in sales for several national organizations before starting her own sales coaching company and teaching her proprietary Selling-Without- Selling method to others.

She holds a Ph.D. in Organizational Behavior and founded the leading coach-training organization, The Coaching Institute (www.CoachInstitute.com). She is a riveting speaker and engaging coach who loves to shift organizations and their sales teams to learn how to sell with ease and give up the old, traditional sales methods that don't work with today's smart consumers. She believes in selling from the heart and simply helping people to do what they love to do—buy!